Self Imposed Chaos

A M G

BookLeaf Publishing

Presentation by *BookLeaf Publishing*

Web: www.bookleafpub.com

E-mail: info@bookleafpub.com

ISBN: 9789357617604

First edition 2022

Artist

Someone once told me:
you don't feel things the same way others do;
as an artist, feeling is more overwhelming.

I do not paint and I do not draw.
I do not create things with my hands;
nor do I capture the raw emotions of humanity
in a single snapshot.

I simply put words to paper, so that I may
continue to exist.
So that the unrelenting sensitivity I have to
everything,
relents for a time and I can carry on being.

I do not consider myself an artist.
Sometimes I may have a way with words,
but it is a direct result of this battle.

My survival is the outcome of these written
sedatives.

Splendour

Bathe in the splendour of your own light.

What does that even mean?
What would it look like?
What does my light look like?

Shady probably. Shady with a silver lining maybe.
Like smoke, smoke and mirrors.
A wisp of the light breaking through, in a flash, and only if you look in just the right way.
How beautiful.
Like sunlight streaking through the clouds.
But just a flash. Just a moment. If you look in just the right way.

A streak through the smoke.
What is that smoke?
Where is it coming from?
There can only be one source.

Fire. Fire within.

I feel you there. I feel you burning deep within.
Making me uncomfortable.

Making me writhe.
Making me itch to be out of my own skin.

The splendour of my own light is a raging inferno.
Angry and unyielding. Indignant.
My splendour is a dangerous, terrible thing.
If I were to bathe in it, tragedy would surely ensue.
If I were to own it, stoke it, encourage it - a maelstrom would raze through the world.
Totally uncontainable.
Completely unleashed on humanity.

What Are You Looking For?

Seduce my mind and you can have my body;
Tell me all the pretty words I want to hear
and I'll give to you this shell,
this flesh.
Win me over with flattery and false promises.
I'll fake ignorance for the opportunity to get lost
in the lie
– in an attempt to hold on to the hope that
keeps me going –
the chance that something more exists.
For one breath, one heart beat, one moment in
time
  I will be yours
    and then I will walk away from you –
      still hollow.

Touch my soul and you can have me for eternity.
You will no longer be just you, but rather
every person, every thing, every experience that
I have felt, moved, loved.
I will give to you that which connects me to the
universe.
There will be a place for you in the dreams of
the waking world.
Like fingers slip together

my heart will slide in hand with yours.
Quietly. Calmly.
  Courage is my faith.
    Courage.
    Coeur.

Weaver

Time is funny.

Weaving its tapestry of lives.

Up and down, back and forth, criss crossing as it marches on.

If I had reached my hand out I would have touched you. A thousand times.

How did two lives wrap around one another for so long without intertwining? And is
that what's finally happening? Or will we simply be pulled past each other again -
destined to remain two separate threads?

The Line

You knock on my door. I'm expecting you but my heart is still pounding.

I know why you're here.

I am still trying to decide if I'm going to let this happen. Foolishly pretending that I'm not teetering over the ledge. That the decision hasn't already been made.

And even as I open the door I still tell myself that it's not something more.

I'm lying of course. We both know there is something more going on here.

You're there. You're so close I could touch you. And for the first time ever, I truly could touch you. I could reach my fingers out and draw them down the length of your jaw; kiss your mouth, taste you, drink you in; let my caution, my discretion slip away. I could throw myself into your arms and no one would know any better.

But I haven't.

This is the line - right here - and neither of us has crossed it.

Yet.

Just a day in the life of…

Always on the go:
Leaving everything 'til the last minute,
Like usual.
Yesterday was chaos –
Strategic in theory –
And then it fell apart.

Choices

That moment when you realize you have to choose:

Be you.
As authentic and raw as you are.
As real and messy and ablaze as you have always been.
Totally loose and unleashed on the world.

Or

Put her in a box.
Lock it as tightly as you can
-forever-
and pray to the heavens that she never escapes.

Wild One

Please stop.

I know that you're there,
  that you're afraid,
    that you can't breathe.

I put you there –
to die.

The sooner you stop railing against me,
            the better.

I can't fit into the box if you exist
and I don't know where my place is if it's not in
one of these boxes.

I struggle with you every day.
  I have always struggled with you
    because the world isn't made for you.

It doesn't care about your knowledge, your
experiences, your opinions.
It's tired of being constantly challenged.

Things don’t work that way;
there’s a glass ceiling that you keep trying to break,
that you don’t respect,
won’t accept.

So I've put you there
because this way
  only one of us has to die,
    and it has to be: you.

I am a rock

I am functional.
I am enduring.
I am constant.

I am a rock.

But you are the water that leeches in,
freezes, and
breaks me.

Hope

When I look across this barren wasteland, I
should see nothing.
It should be empty.
Void.
Dead.
When I look across this barren wasteland, I
should be able to turn away and forget it ever
existed.
Nothing left to hold me here.
Nothing to remind me.
Nothing.

So simple.

But there
-way out there-
in the centre of this desolation
is something.
Something terrible.
Something so insignificant that it should hardly
matter.
An unseeable sliver buried beneath the skin of
this place.

A sliver.

Infection
spreading beneath the surface.
Red and angry.
Weeping with the corpses of the warriors who
fought against it.
Crippling me
one breath at a time.
Invasive. Corrosive.

I hate this disease.

A Message

crack

I have been robbed –
the air I breathe is gone.
Confusion overwhelmed and distracted
so that Shock could hold me captive
and then Pain snuck in to steal it away.

My world begins to crumble
and Reason starts laying the bricks
of the wall that is our divide.
Thought betrayed us, and now
we're caught in the trap Fear set.

But then suddenly the air returned.
Belief had made a chink in the wall
and Hope slipped in with a message
from my Heart: *he'll be back –*
I know something you don't.

War Zone

Dear one
How did you get here?
Barren creeks
Twisted, lifeless trees
Parched earth
Where is this terrible landscape?

Here
Take my hand
I have a small shelter I can share with you
It's not much
But here we can be safe
While we plan your way out
Here you can gather your strength
And once you are ready,
We will go

I can feel the terror outside
Hear a blast
See an explosion
Taste the poison
It's time to go or else we will both become trapped here

One step
Safe if we focus
Two
We must be careful
Thre-
    SHRAPNEL
Four
Pull the metal out of our skin
Fi-
    BURNS
Six
Wrap the wounds
Seven
Hold on
Eigh-
    GAS

Bomb after bomb they go off
I turn to you in concern
And realize
  you're holding
    the detonator.

Drinking the Kool-aid

a long time ago i came to terms with the
knowledge that i'm not special.
i'm not unique.
not different.
and that's okay.
but
-if that's the case-
how did i become so infutiatingly lost?
when did i lose sight of the vision?
did i do this to myself
by accepting a truth that wasn't meant for me?

The Stranger

I keep questioning my life.
Always questions -
as if I'm not the only expert there is on me;
as if anyone else is going to be able to answer
them.

How did I get here?

I put myself here.
I told myself that I'm not special, not unique,
not as vast as I feel.
I obeyed the world when it told me not to make
waves
and now I'm confused about why my craft isn't
going anywhere.

Why did I allow this to happen?

Because I am afraid.
I'm afraid that the fire I feel is misleading me, is
as out of control as I've been led to believe.
And if I am not in control, then there is no way
for me to mitigate the damage caused by living.
To prevent the heart break, avoid the grief, stop
the loss.

When did I lose myself?

And who did I become instead?

Control

breathe in
breathe out
contract
expand
hold
release

i am a breath.
i am not my breath.
i am not not alive because of breath.
i am breath.

i began as the universe.
i began as endless possibility.
i began as all the fight and passion and knowledge that exists.
i began -
to contract.

with each thought, and each look, and each word.
slowly closing in on myself.
smaller.
  and smaller.
    and smaller.

now, i am unobtrusive.
now, i fit into the mold.
now, i am safe.
now, i - hold.
wait.
stop.

break

before i can collect all the pieces back up, i'm
seeping out through the cracks.
out into the world.
into a world that can't handle me.
doesn't want to.
but i can't breathe in any further,
the release is out of my control.
i expand.

now, i'm a stranger in my own life.
i've built it too small,
too agreeable,
too insignificant.
i don't know how to reconcile with the fire
inside.

instead -
  i burn.

Hysterical

I haven't done anything wrong.
Why would I apologize when I haven't done anything wrong?
I will not be
  accused,
  silenced,
  wronged,
  attacked,
    and not defend myself.
Not ever.
And I will not apologize for your bad behaviour.
It is not my responsibility.
It is not -my- responsibility to manage -your- emotions;
especially when I have gone out of my way to ensure I have delivered myself clearly, genuinely, respectfully.
If we're having a serious discussion, I'm going to treat it like a serious discussion.
  I'm going to have serious feelings about it;
    I'm going to ask serious questions;
      and I'm going to use
          serious
          communication.

I want to be sure I understand very clearly
what's going on,
  so I know how to respond,
  so I know what to change,
  so I know the trigger;
and I deserve to be understood as intended.
If you misunderstand me, I will focus on
ensuring you understand exactly what I
need you to.
And why shouldn't I?
If it's so blatantly obvious to me that you don't
understand, do you really expect me
to just let you carry on?
Lost in your toxic narrative?
Drinking the water of some mirage?
Grasping at long dead stars?
You don't have to agree, but I will not stand by
while you put words in my mouth -
  or worse,   feelings in my heart.
If you can hardly understand your own feelings,
how dare you think you can dictate
mine.

Universe

i am a well so deep you can't even fathom my bottom.
that you have no respect for the universe exploding within these depths eats away at me.
how can we ever last if you don't appreciate the wild sleeping beside you?

NDA

NDA… NDA… NDA

Nailed Down Abruptly

No voice
Disrespected
Again

Nothing – Done – Appropriately

Non Discloser Agreement

It's laughable.
Absolutely hysterical!
That you think, the insignificant disgrace you are,
could EVER be powerful enough to silence me.

What a joke.

Just because I'm not allowed to say the words
doesn't mean I can't speak.
Do you think my silence doesn't have its own message?

That my eyes are mute?
That my expressions remain blank?
That my body does not tell a story?
Do you really believe that I would let others in my position walk into your perdition without issuing my own kind of warning?

Silly   little   man.

I am woman.
Hear me
  -roar.

Daydreamer

I trace my way by heart.
Each tree, each rock, each twist in the path
are as old to me as time
and I no longer recall their dawn in my world.
I hear the wind drift through new leaves
and feel the soft ground under my feet.
Soon I have arrived.

As always, my spot awaits me.
Like a Queen to her throne,
I take my place upon the smooth stone surface;
a perch from which I can observe my realm.
Endless fields of green
stretch out across miles of rolling hills
and golden sunshine splays over them
from a vast blue sky.
I breathe in the scent of spring
– thankful for my hidden world –
and breathe out the stress of the day.

But wait –
something is coming,
something ominous.
Creeping towards me
they mar the picture.

As the wind begins to blow
it drives the dark clouds closer and closer,
their shadows marching across the landscape.

drip
Determined to save the moment
drop
I quibble with Mother Nature,
drip
but it is no use –
she is unwavering.

Water cascades from the sky.

The rain fall is ferocious.
Within moments I am soaked to the bone.
My jacket has become an afterthought,
no more able to return that sweet moment than
I am.

Admitting defeat I retrace my steps.
Each twist, each rock, each tree:
now a soggy mess.
Tomorrow I shall return;
for my realm awaits
and as its Queen I am devoted.

Selves

It’s okay to have boundaries.
Don’t let anyone waste your time.
Be fierce and strong and soft.

Practice. Self. Care.

At what point is my “self care” destroying my
life? At what point is it time to suck it
up, and get shit done? At what point is it time to
stop being selfish and start being
selfless?

The world cannot revolve around selves. Self
care is going to destroy us.

We must unlearn this individualism. We must
rediscover our communities. We must
come back to our humanity.

This New Morning

This new morning… I will find all that I seek.
I will breathe and climb and search for what I need.
I will take the view around me deep into my lungs – into my soul.
I will look out upon it, brimming with possibility and beauty and the intensity of it all.
And when I'm done, when I lower myself back down to the world, I will rest.
Boxed in by flesh and furr, black, brown, and white.
My heart will relax as the experiences of life settle themselves into their spaces.
As we stretch and purr and grumble with one another,
we slide into connection and creation together.
Even if we don't know what we're doing.

www.ingramcontent.com/pod-product-compliance
Lightning Source LLC
Chambersburg PA
CBHW062204160726
48282CB00027B/995
* 9 7 8 9 3 5 7 6 1 7 6 0 4 *